Children's Sermons
with Humor

Children's Sermons with Humor

By the Hilarious Miss Polly

Mary Phillips

To order additional copies of this book, contact:
Xlibris Corporation
1-888-795-4274
www.Xlibris.com
Orders@Xlibris.com
58784

CONTENTS

Dedicated to
My two dear grandchildren,
Sean and Olivia

INTRODUCTION

Do you ever find yourself losing the children's attention? I have developed the original idea of Miss Polly to convey God's message in a comical fashion. I disguised myself as an elderly, uneducated, hillbilly lady who loves the Lord. The positive response from both children and adults has been overwhelming. Each lesson contains scripture and a biblical message with insertions of humor. Each message concludes with a short prayer.

Miss Polly can be created by anyone. I wear a shaggy gray wig, sunglasses, and a large brimmed bright pink hat topped with an artificial sunflower. Make sure that you wear those ugly hillbilly teeth that can be purchased at any costume store. Wearing those teeth also helps you to talk more with a hillbilly slang. I am slim, so I wear a cushion under the back of a gaudy old dress to make my hips appear large. I wear gloves and non-matching beads and always make sure that my slip is showing. Hose are rolled below my knees with colored bobby socks and big string-up work shoes on my feet. You will have people laughing even before you start your sermon.

In Lesson 9, I introduce Miss Polly's husband, Henry. With this lesson, I used a picture of my husband dressed in a funny mask, burned it on a disc, and showed it on a large screen on the sanctuary wall. Another option would be to have an actual person appear in costume. You can use the same method with Lesson 10 where I introduce their son, Odbert, and Lessons 17 and 18 where their daughter, Sadie, is introduced. Also, in

Lesson 17 where I introduced the family cat, I used one of those funny cat pictures from a greeting card.

Remember, Miss Polly has only been through second grade. Therefore, her grammar and pronunciations are poor and in hillbilly slang. You will be amazed at how the children and adults give Miss Polly their undivided attention and remember her messages. These sermons can be used during a worship service, for Sunday School openings, church camps, vacation bible schools, or youth meetings.

The purpose of this book is to draw boys and girls closer to God, give them laughter, and help them to realize that it can be fun to learn about God and his principles.

1

Salvation and Baptism

John 3:16 For God so loved the world, that he gave his only begotten Son, that whosoever believeth in him should not perish, but have everlasting life. KJV

Howdy boys and girls. My name is Miss Polly. I got all dressed up for you today. I wore my new hat and my new shoes. I got these shoes at the Farm & Country Store. They're the latest fashion. I even brushed my teeth this morning, all three of them. I've always had such pretty teeth. That's why I take good care of them and brush them every week. You boys and girls remember that. Brush your teeth every week. Then you will have pretty teeth like mine.

Do any of you boys and girls go to school? I used to go to school. I went all the way through the second grade. Four times. My mama was so proud of me. She said, "Your teacher must really love you to keep you in her second grade class four years in a row." I said, "Yes, and sometimes she even has me to stay after class." Now my first grade teacher, I don't think that she liked me very well 'cause I was only in the first grade for two years. But my second grade teacher really loved me. She even wanted me to be in her class for five years, but I thanked her and told her that I was sorry that I couldn't spend another year with her 'cause I was going to have to stay home and help my mama and papa on the farm. I fed the chickens and milked the cows.

Me and my family went to church every Sunday, and I probably learned more in Sunday School than I did in all of my years in second grade. My preacher told me that all I needed to remember was that Jesus loved me and that God loved me so much that He sent his son Jesus to die on the cross for my sins. That's in the Bible, in John 3:16, and it says that whoever believes in Him will not perish but have everlasting life. I believed and I asked Jesus to come into my heart. My preacher told me that I had just done the most important thing that I would ever do in my whole life. Then I was baptized in a "crick." When I was telling someone this the other day, he asked, "What on earth is a "crick?" I'm thinking, boy, this guy must not have went past first grade; but I was very nice and explained to him that a crick is water that runs over rocks. It's like a baby river that's deep enough to wade in. Then me and my preacher waded out into that "crick," and he asked me if I loved Jesus and if I believed that Jesus was the son of God and died on the cross for my sins; and I said, "Yes sir, I do." Then he baptized me in the name of the Father, Son, and Holy Spirit. I'm not sure how old I was when I was baptized but I know I was in the second grade, I think the fourth time.

Then he said, "Now, Polly, do you know how you can show Jesus that you love him?" I said, "How's that, preacher?" He said, "By keeping God's commandments; by being good." I said, "Okay," and that's why I always try to be good, so that Jesus will know that I love him. Let's bow our heads now for a little prayer.

Prayer: Dear Lord, thank you for loving us so much. Help us to please you in all that we do. In Jesus' name we pray. Amen.

2

Sitting Still In Church

Proverbs 22:6 Train up a child in the way he should go:
and when he is old, he will not depart from it. KJV

Howdy boys and girls. It's good to see you again. I washed my hair last night. It was Saturday night. Now it won't lay down. It just wants to stick out everywhere. I tried spittin' on it, but it still doesn't lay down very well. I'm thinking about getting one of those "permits." You know one of those curly "permits" at the beauty "saloon." What do you boys and girls think? I'm thinking about it.

I'm going to tell you a story about something that happened to me when I was in second grade. Remember, I was in the second grade for four years, so a lot happened to me when I was in second grade. This story is about something that my Mama taught me at church.

We went to a little country church and I would sit beside my Mama. She would keep telling me to sit still and listen to the preacher. I just kept listening for him to stop talkin' so then I knew it would be time to go home. I would put my fingers in the holes where the communion cups went. I took off my shoes and looked at them. I tried to lay down on the seat but my Mama told me to sit up. Then I started trying to count the blocks on the ceiling, but I forgot and started countin' out loud. Then my Mama said, "Let's go outside." I thought, oh good, I get to go outside.

But when we got outside, I saw that it wasn't good 'cause my Mama was mad. She said, "I told you to sit still and listen to the preacher." She then sit down on the step and turned me across her knee and whacked me good on my bottom. I think it's still swollen. (point to padded hips) She then asked, "Do you think that you can sit still now?" I answered, "I hope that I can still sit down Mama." Then I told her that I was sorry and I would try real hard to sit still and listen to the preacher. And you know what? I'm glad that my Mama made me sit still and listen 'cause I found out that the preacher was saying some pretty interesting things. Most of the time I understood everything he was talkin' about. Sometimes, he would tell a funny story about his life. Then he would talk about people in the Bible and tell us what God wanted us to do.

I hadn't realized what I had been missin'. My Mama was right. It was a lot better sittin' still and listenin' to the preacher. Besides, countin' those squares on the ceiling got real "frustrationings." I think that's the word. Those big long words just get all tangled up all around my teeth. You boys and girls remember to sit still and listen to the preacher so you won't get taken outside like I was. Let's bow our heads for prayer.

Prayer: Dear Lord, thank you for Mamas that show us what is best for us and thank you for the preachers that tell us about you and your son, Jesus. In Jesus' name we pray. Amen.

3

The Golden Rule

*Matthew 7:12 Do to others what you would
have them do to you. NIV*

(Wearing dark surgery glasses) Howdy boys and girls. Wait just a minute. (pointing to some man in the congregation) Is that you Cousin Elwood? You look a lot like my Cousin Elwood. But I can't see too good today. I just had surgery on my eyes. I had cadillacs. I was talking to some man the other day and he said that he was going to buy a Cadillac. I said, "I wish I had known that 'cause I just got rid of two of them." He said, "You had two cadillacs?" I said, "Yes, the one on the right eye was a little worse than the one on the left."

You know boys and girls, I have never told you my last name. My last name is Parrot. (pronounce "pair-rot") It is spelled the same as parrot. One time when I was in second grade and I was outside playin', two mean boys started callin' me names. They said, "Polly Parrot, she mocks everything that you say. Does Polly want a cracker?" I said that my name is not parrot. My name is Par-rot (pair-rot). They mocked me more and said, "So you are a rotten pear. Does Polly Parrot want a rotten pear?" I seen that I was getting no where, and I was startin' to get tears in my eyes, and I did not want them to see me cryin'. So, I just walked away and went to the bathroom and wiped away my tears.

Then I went to the other side of the playground to play with some nice kids.

The next day, I saw those same two mean boys calling another girl named Harriet names. Harriet was overweight. So, they were calling her "fatty" and "piggy" and Harriet was cryin'. I felt sorry for her 'cause I knew just how she felt. So I went inside and told the teacher that Harriet was cryin' 'cause those two boys were calling her names. My teacher, Miss Wilson, came outside and she heard those two mean boys saying, "Fatty Harriet is a crybaby." Miss Wilson then walked over to the two boys and said, "I need to see you two boys in my room." When she took them in her room, she said, "I do not allow anyone to be bullies in my class. I do not allow anyone to call other kids names, but everyone is to treat each other with respect. I want to make sure that you boys remember this lesson, so both of you lean over my desk." Then she took her big wooden paddle from a nail on the wall and gave each of the boys two big whacks. When they came out of the room, they had tears coming down their cheeks. Did I call them "crybabies?" No, but I couldn't help but have a little smile on my face.

When we came back into the classroom, Miss Wilson taught a lesson that I will always remember. It wasn't from a textbook, but it was from the Bible. She said that in Matthew 7:12, Jesus said, 'Do unto others as you would have them do unto you.' She said that this is the Golden Rule and I want all of you boys and girls to practice this. She said that you have heard it quoted that sticks and stones will break my bones but words will never hurt me. That is not true. Sticks and stones can hurt for a few minutes but words can hurt for a long time, sometimes forever. So, everybody was nicer after that.

So, boys and girls, let's try to remember this Golden Rule and always try to treat other people nice. Let's bow our heads for prayer.

Prayer: Dear Lord, thank you for the Golden Rule that shows us how to treat others. In Jesus' name we pray. Amen.

4

Witnessing

Acts 1:8b 'and you will be my witnesses in Jerusalem, and in all Judea and Samaria, and to the ends of the earth." NIV

Howdy, boys and girls. I went to the dentist last week. He told me to open my mouth wide so that he could look at my teeth. I said, "Why do you want me to open my mouth, doctor? They're all three sticking out right here." He said, "Do you brush after meals?" I said, "No, I brush before." 'Cause I always brush all three of them before breakfast on Sunday mornings. He said, "I've never see any teeth like these before." I could tell that he was pretty impressed 'cause then he went and got his assistant to come and look at my teeth. I was feelin' pretty proud and I told him that I'd had these teeth since I was in second grade. He said, "Have you ever considered getting dentures or a partial?" I didn't know what he was talking about. So, I said, "No, do you think I need some?" He said, "You sure do." I said, "Then in that case, I'll take three of each." So I don't know what I'm getting.

I want to tell you boys and girls about something else that happened to me when I was in second grade. One Sunday, our preacher said that he wanted us to witness to others about Jesus. So, the next day at school while we were eating lunch, I began telling some kids about Jesus. The first girl walked away. But then a little girl named Jenny said, "I would like to hear more about Jesus, Polly." I told her all I could remember. I told her about church and how I asked Jesus into my heart and some day I would go to Heaven. Jenny said that she would like to go to church, but she didn't think that her parents would take her. I said, "Me and my Mama and Papa will pick you up and take you to church with us, if it's okay with your Mama." She said, "I'll ask her and let you know tomorrow."

Her Mama told her yes. So, we picked her up every Sunday. One day, Jenny went up front and told the preacher that she wanted to ask Jesus into her heart. Then she was baptized in that same "crick" that I was baptized in. Jenny and I became best friends.

One day Jenny said, "Polly, you won't have to pick me up for church on Sunday." I said, "Why not, Jenny, that's too far for you to walk?" She was smiling and she said, "No, I'm not walking. My Mommy and Daddy are going to church with me." So then, they started coming with her every Sunday.

My preacher came up to me later and said, "See Polly, how witnessing works. You witnessed to Jenny and now she and her whole family are in church. The love of Jesus is contagious." I said, "You mean like the measles?" He said, "Well sort of, Polly. You just keep on witnessing." I said, "Okay," and here I am after all these years still witnessing to you boys and girls. So, you boys and girls try telling other kids about Jesus and see if you can get someone like Jenny to come to church with you. Now, let's bow our heads for a little prayer.

Prayer: Dear Lord, help us to tell others about your son, Jesus. In Jesus' name. Amen.

5

The Bible (God's Love Letter)

2 Timothy 3:16 All Scripture is God-breathed ...NIV

Howdy boys and girls. This morning I'm going to tell you about something that I learned in Sunday School when I was in second grade. One morning my Sunday School teacher said that we were going to talk about the most important book in the world and almost every family in the United States had one of these books. She said, "It is my favorite book. Can someone tell me what that book is?" Well, my hand went right up 'cause I knew the answer to that. My teacher said, "Okay, Polly, can you tell us what book we are talking about?" I said, "Yes, teacher, I think it is the Sears & Roebuck catalog." She said, "Well, that's not what I had in mind." Then she went on to explain about the Bible.

She said that the Bible was written over a period of about 1500 years by 44 different people. These people wrote this under God's "inspiratorationings." I think that's the word. It's one of those big long words that gets all tangled up all around my teeth. It means that God inspired these people to write these words. The Bible is divided into two sections, the old testament and the new testament. There are 66 books in the Bible. All of these books tie together from the beginning to the end. All of these books come together to make one big book. Isn't God amazing? My teacher said that the Bible is God's love letter to us. I said,

"Teacher, God must really love us a lot 'cause this sure is a long letter."
She said, "God does love us a lot. That is why we should all be sure and
read His Book, the Bible."

My Sunday School teacher was right. The Bible is the best book in
the world and it's my favorite book now, too. I hope that you boys and
girls will remember to take time every day to read some of God's Book.
Let's bow our heads now for a little prayer.

Prayer: Dear God, thank you for your long love letter to us and we will
show our love to you by reading your Book, the Bible. In Jesus' name
we pray. Amen.

6

The Real Meaning of Christmas

Matthew 25:40 The King will reply, 'I tell you the truth, whatever you did for one of the least of these brothers of mine, you did for me.' NIV

Howdy boys and girls. Since it is Christmas time, I wore a bell around my neck. (pointing at cowbell around neck) I borrowed this from Bessie. Bessie is my cow. Miss Debbie (or name of someone in congregation), you can borrow this anytime you want to. I brought all of you kids a candy cane today. (pass them out) I remember when I was in first grade on one Christmas morning, I hollered downstairs and asked Mama, "Did Santa bring me anything?" She said, "He brought you a cane." I'm thinking what do I need a cane for, I can walk fine; I don't have a broken leg or anything. It was a cane like this. (hold up a candy cane) When I saw the cane, I said, "It's a good thing that I don't have a broken leg. This little cane sure wouldn't do me any good." Mama said, "Oh Polly, it's a candy cane. You are supposed to eat it." So, then I liked it. My favorite Christmas present when I was in first grade was my two front teeth. I've still got 'em. I think they wrote a song about that later.

This morning, I'm going to tell you a story that happened when I was in second grade. You remember, my second grade teacher really liked me, so I got to stay in her class for four years. This was at Christmas time, and at church the preacher asked us kids what we liked best about Christmas. One boy said all of the presents, a girl said the Christmas tree, one said all the lights, one said Santa Claus, and one said all the food and candy. When it came to my turn, I said, "Preacher, I don't know." He said, "I know that all of this is can be very "confutioning." I think that's the word. Those big long words get all tangled up all around my teeth. Then he told us what Christmas is all about. He said that Jesus was born as a little baby. Jesus is God's son. Jesus' mother, her name was Mary, put little baby Jesus in a manger 'cause she didn't have a baby bed. Then he talked about the Shepherds and Wise Men who came to see baby Jesus. He said the reason that we have Christmas is because it is Jesus' birthday. Well, I was still "confutioned" because I couldn't understand. If it was Jesus' birthday, why were we getting all the presents?

The next week, I went to school and we were practicing for our Christmas program. My friend Jenny had the leading role. She sang good and had a lot of lines. I was in it too. I was a reindeer. On Friday, after practice I seen that Jenny looked sad. I went to her and said, "What's wrong, Jenny? You are doing a great job with your part." She said, "My Mama won't get to come and watch me in the program tomorrow night." I said, "Why Jenny, is she sick?" She said, "No, we don't have much money this year. My Mama bought my brother and me new coats and new shoes this year for school, but she didn't have enough money to buy shoes for herself. She doesn't have any shoes. When she goes outside to feed the chickens, she wears my Dad's four-buckle artic boots; and she doesn't want to wear those to the school play 'cause people would make fun of her." Then I don't know why I asked but I said, "What size shoe does she wear?" She said, "A seven." I was thinking that was the same size I wore. When I was little, I used to have big feet. So, when I got home after school, my Mama said, "Polly, I got you something new to wear in the school Christmas program tomorrow night, a new pair of shoes." I looked at them. They were real "purty" shoes, but then I thought about Jenny's Mama not having any shoes. So I said to my Mama, "These are really "purty" shoes, but Jenny's Mama doesn't have any shoes, and my old shoes are still okay. Would it be okay with you if I gave these shoes to Jenny's Mama?" My Mama got a little smile and with tears in her eyes she said, "Polly, those are your shoes and you can do with them whatever you want to." So, I said, "Can I take them over to Jenny's now?" My

Mama couldn't drive, so she said, "As soon as your Papa comes home, he can drive you over."

So, when me and Papa drove up to Jenny's house, Jenny was going up the walk and I hollered at her. I ran up to her and handed her the box of shoes and said, "Jenny, this is for your Mama." She took the lid off of the box and when she saw the shoes, she had tears in her eyes and she hugged me. She said, "Thank you, Polly, you are the best friend in the world." I had a real warm feeling right there in my heart. (point to chest)

The next night at the school program, Jenny was singing real good. I was up there too; remember 'cause I was a reindeer. I looked back and saw Jenny's Mama watching Jenny with a smile on her face. I looked at her feet and saw the shoes that I gave her, and I got that real warm feeling in my heart again. After the program, we all went to a hospital and sang Christmas carols. There were people there in beds and in wheelchairs, and when they heard us singing they smiled and had tears in their eyes. I got that warm feeling in my heart again.

The next morning at church I was thinking about those warm feelings I had in my heart. So, I went up to the preacher and said, "I know now what I like best about Christmas." He said, "What is that, Polly?" I said, "What I like best about Christmas is making other people happy." He said, "Polly, I think that you have just discovered the true meaning of Christmas. I am very proud of you." Then when he got up to preach, he mentioned my name in the sermon. My Mama was real proud of me. The preacher said, "Polly has told me that what she likes best about Christmas is making other people happy. That is what Christmas is all about. It is not about getting but it's about giving. Jesus said in Matthew 25:40 that when we give to others in need that we are giving to him."

So, I have always loved Christmas and I wanted to give you boys and girls something today. I hope that you like your candy canes and have a very Merry Christmas. Let's bow our heads for prayer.

Prayer: Dear Lord, thank you for Christmas, and please help us to remember that the best way to celebrate Jesus' birthday is by giving to others. In Jesus' name we pray. Amen.

7

Tithing

Luke 6:38 "Give, and it will be given to you. A good measure, pressed down, shaken together and running over, will be poured into your lap. For with the measure you use, it will be measured to you." NIV

Malachi 3:8 "Will a man rob God? Yet you rob me. But you ask,' How do we rob you?' "In tithes and offerings." NIV

Howdy boys and girls. I want to tell you about my first job. Remember, we lived on a farm. So, when I was 12 years old, I put a stand along side the road and sold corn. I also sold "maters" and "taters." I sold maters, taters, and corn. I gave all the money to my Papa and then he would pay me for sittin' at the stand.

The first time I got paid, my Mama asked, "Now Polly, do you know what the first thing is that you are supposed to do with your money?" I said, "Hide it?" She said, "No, you are to give one tenth of it to God." I'm wonderin' how on earth I'm going to do that. I said, "But Mama, I don't know his address." She explained that the church is God's house and that God wants us to give our ten percent, which is called tithes to the church.

Then she got out her Bible and she read to me out of the book of Malachi; and it said that if we don't give one tenth of everything that we receive to the church, then we are robbing God. Then she read this verse from Luke 6:38. "Give, and it will be given to you. A good measure, pressed down, shaken together and running over, will be poured into your lap. For with the measure you use, it will be measured to you."

Well my first question was: What are they going to pour into my lap? Then Mama explained that this means that God has promised us that if we are generous in giving to Him that he will give us back much more than we have given. You can never out give God. He just keeps giving back to us. Isn't God good? Let's bow our heads for prayer.

Prayer: Dear Lord, thank you for your promises. Help us to always be generous in our tithes and offerings to you. In Jesus' name we pray. Amen.

8

Clean Language

Colossians 3:8 But now you must rid yourselves of all such things as these: anger, rage, malice, slander, and filthy language from your lips. NIV

James 3:10 Out of the same mouth come praise and cursing. My brothers, this should not be. NIV

Howdy boys and girls. I'm going to tell you a story today about my cousin Elwood. I don't have a picture of Elwood. Poor Elwood, he wasn't good-looking like the rest of our family. My cousin Elwood was visiting one day. Me and Elwood were racing. I could run pretty fast, 'specially when I wasn't wearing shoes. Elwood was ahead of me, but suddenly he tripped over a rock and fell down. I ran ahead and won the race. Then I came back and checked on Elwood. He had skinned up his knee and he was mad. He said some bad words. I won't tell you what they were, but he was cussin'. My Mama and his Mama were sitting on the porch and they heard what Elwood said. His Mama took him in the house. First, she washed off his knee and put some "curecomb" on it. Then she said, "Elwood, I heard some words come out of your mouth that should not have come out of there. Now, I'm going to wash those dirty words out of your mouth." She got a bar of soap and washed out

Elwood's mouth. He bubbled for an hour after that. It looked like the Lawrence Welk Show.

Then she got out the Bible and read him these verses. "But now you must rid yourselves of all such things as these: anger, rage, malice, slander, and filthy language from your lips." Colossians 3:8. Out of the mouth come praise and cursing, . . . this should not be. James 3:10. I never heard my cousin Elwood cuss anymore after that. Let's bow our heads now for prayer.

Prayer: Dear Lord, please help us to never say bad words, but always keep our words clean. In Jesus' name we pray. Amen.

9

Jesus' Bride

Revelation 19:9 ... 'Blessed are those who are invited
to the wedding supper of the Lamb!' NIV

Howdy boys and girls. Since it is the week of Valentine's Day, I'm going to tell you about my sweetheart. His name is Henry. I brought his picture. This is me and Henry. (show picture) Ain't he handsome? When I was about 18, I met Henry at church. He started walking me home after church. He would hold my hand. Then one night he asked, "Polly, do you think that it would be alright if I kissed you good night?" I said, "I think that would be fine." So, he smacked me a big kiss right on the mouth. I'll never forget it. There was blood everywhere. It cut his lip wide open. His lip bled for an hour after that. Ever since then, he just kisses me on the cheek.

Later, Henry and I got married. We've been married for 47 years. I remember when the preacher said, "I now pronounce you man and wife. Henry, you may kiss the bride." Henry said, "Do I have to?" I knew what he was thinkin', so I pointed to my cheek and he kissed me on the cheek, 'cause I didn't want to get blood all over my white dress.

When we said our wedding vows to love, honor, and obey, it reminded me of when I asked Jesus into my heart and I promised to love, honor, and obey Jesus forever. When we accept Jesus into our heart, we become

28

a part of God's church. Did you know that God's church is going to be Jesus' bride? In the Bible in Revelation Chapter 19, it talks about Jesus' wedding. It says that as God's church, we will be marrying Jesus and we will be invited to the wedding supper. You know that everything that God does is far greater and better than anything that we can imagine. Well, I can hardly wait to see what God is going to serve us to eat at that wedding supper. It is going to be some feast. If we have asked Jesus into our heart, we will all be there 'cause we're going to be the bride. Isn't that exciting?

Remember before, I told you that my name used to be Polly Parrot (pronounced Pair-rot), and all the kids called me Polly Parrot. But after I married Henry, my name changed. Now I have a wonderful name. Henry's name is Henry Wolly. So, now my name is Polly Wolly. So, see boys and girls, things always turn out good. Let's bow our heads for a little prayer.

Prayer: Dear Lord, thank you for all of your promises in the Bible and help us to always show you our love by obeying you. And Lord, we sure are looking forward to that Wedding Supper. In Jesus' name. Amen.

10

Honor Your Father and Mother

Exodus 20:12 Honor your father and mother. so that you may live long in the land the Cord your God is giving you. NIV

Howdy boys and girls. Remember, I was telling you about my husband, Henry. Well, Henry and me have a son. I want to show you his picture. We named him Odbert. We call him Odd for short. That's his nickname, Odd. You young ladies look at this picture 'cause he is still single. He's smart. He went all the way through sixth grade. I went all the way through second grade and Henry went through the fourth grade. Since Odd went all the way through sixth grade, he said that he knew as much as me and his Pa put together. I told him to remember the Fifth Commandment that says to Honor your Father and Mother if he wanted to have a long life.

He's always been a good boy. When I'd tell him to clean his room, he'd clean it right up. When his Pa asked him to help feed the cows, he never complained. When he would see the grass getting high, he would just go out and mow it. He's always been good.

One day, I asked Odd, "How come you've always been such a good boy? How come you have never given me or your Pa any trouble?" He said, "Well, I always remember that time that you threatened my life if I didn't honor you and Pa." I said, "What on earth are you talkin' about, Odd. I have never threatened your life." He said, "Ma, you said that I was

30

to honor you and Pa if I wanted to have a long life." I said, "Odd, honey, I wasn't threatenin' your life. I was just quotin' scripture. In the Bible, God promises us that if we honor our father and mother, He will give us a long life." He said, "Oh, okay Ma. That's a relief." Then he said, "Well, that's okay. I liked being good to you and Pa anyway 'cause I love ya." So see, he really is a good boy.

Odd has always helped us do a lot of work on the farm. One day, I told him that with all of his education that he should be able to get a good job, and he did. He got a real good job. He works part time at a hotdog stand.

So, you boys and girls remember to study hard in school and to honor your father and mother and you will have a long life. And, that's not a threat. That's God's promise in Exodus 20:12. Let's bow our heads for a little prayer.

Prayer: Dear Lord, thank you for our parents. Help us to always honor and respect them. In Jesus' name we pray. Amen.

11

Stealing

Exodus 20:15 Thou shalt not steal. KJV

Howdy boys and girls. I went to my cousin Elwood's wedding last week. Do you remember me telling you about Elwood? He wasn't blessed with good looks like the rest of us in my family. He is 75 years old and finally found a woman to marry him. She can't see very good. She has "cadillacs" on her eyes. So, they got married. I wore this outfit to the wedding. I cleaned all the mud off of my shoes. You know how I always try to dress nice when I come to church or to a wedding. I couldn't decide which necklace looked right with this dress. So, I just wore all of them. (point at 4 or 5 big necklaces around neck) I figured I couldn't go wrong if I wore them all.

I'm going to tell you another story that happened to me when I was in second grade. You know, compared to you kids today, everyone in our school was poor. Now I wasn't the poorest poor or I wasn't the richest poor. I was kind of medium poor.

When I was in school, I loved to color. That year for school I got a box of crayons that had 64 colors. Most of the kids only had 16 or 24 colors. I was so happy with my 64 color crayons. I kept them in my desk.

Then about a week later, I opened my desk to get my crayons and they weren't there. Someone had taken my crayons. I told the teacher that my crayons were gone. So, that night Miss Wilson, that's my teacher, looked in everyone's desks but she didn't find the crayons. The next morning, she told me that whoever had taken my crayons must have taken them home. The next day, I seen a girl named Nola with a big box of crayons and I told my teacher. Miss Wilson talked to Nola, and Nola said that they were her crayons, but Miss Wilson had me to look at them. I remembered that I had written my name on the side of the box. So, I looked and on the side of the box, Nola had marked out my name and wrote her name above it. I showed Miss Wilson where my name had been written. You couldn't fool Miss Wilson. She knew that the crayons were mine and that Nola was lying. Then Miss Wilson gave me the crayons and took Nola out in the hall. Us kids knew what she was doing. Nola got paddled.

When they came back in the room, Miss Wilson got out the Bible and read us the Ten Commandments. She said, "I want all of you boys and girls to notice the eighth commandment, Thou shall not steal. I will not allow any stealing in this school." Then she said, "Notice the tenth commandment, Thou shall not covet." She said, "That means that you are not to want something that belongs to someone else. If you keep this commandment, then you won't be stealing from others." Poor Nola kept her head down the whole time. I was sorry that she got paddled, but I just wanted my crayons back. I never mentioned it to her again. But at Christmas time, we drew names for exchange presents, and I got Nola's name. Guess what I got her for Christmas? A box of crayons with 64 colors.

You boys and girls remember to never covet something that belongs to someone else, then you won't ever be stealing anything. Let's bow our heads for a little prayer.

Prayer: Dear Lord, thank you for your commandments. Please help us to never steal or desire something that belongs to someone else. In Jesus' name. Amen.

12

Finders Keepers, Losers Weepers

Exodus 20:15 Thou shalt not steal. KJV

Howdy boys and girls. I'm movin' kind of slow today. I got arthritis in my back. Henry says it's 'cause I gained weight. He says if I get any bigger, I'm gonna have to wear a sign on my back that says "Wide Load." The only good thing about walking bent over this way is that you find a lot of lost coins. I found two quarters on the way here this morning. Do you think that I should keep these two quarters? Have you ever heard anyone say, "Finders keepers, losers weepers?" Do you think that is very nice? It's not nice for the person who loses something, is it?

Let me tell you a story that happened when I was in second grade. There was this girl named Gertrude. She was always finding things on the playground and she would always keep them. She would say, "Finders keepers, losers weepers." One day she found a dollar bill on the playground, but she didn't tell the teacher. She just stuck the dollar bill in her pocket. Later, a little boy named Sam said that he had lost a dollar bill that his mother had given him for his lunch money. I told him that Gertrude had found a dollar bill on the playground. So, he told Gertrude that he lost his lunch money and the dollar bill that she found was his. She said, "Well, you can't prove it. So, finders keepers, losers weepers." She refused to give him the dollar.

The next week, do you know what happened? Gertrude had a new birthstone ring that she got for her birthday. She was so proud of it and was showing it to everyone. Later in the day, we heard Gertrude screaming. She had looked at her hand and her ring was missing. She was shouting, "I've lost my beautiful ring. Has anyone found my ring? Please help me look for my ring." The kids started shouting, "Finders keepers, losers weepers." Gertrude had a terrified look on her face 'cause she knew that those were always her words. She said, "Oh no, I will never keep someone else's lost things again."

Gertrude's ring was never found. We think that she probably lost it in the outhouse. That's like a commode. In your school, you kids have two baths. We had two paths; one for the boys and one for the girls. After that, when the kids found something they were always good about giving it to the teacher.

So, do you boys and girls think that I should keep these two quarters that I found this morning? No, I'll try to find who they belong to. What you do when you find something is that you try to find who the owner is. If it happens at school, then you turn it in at the office. So, then the owner can come there to find it. Because if you lost something valuable, that is what you would want someone do for you. Let's remember to never keep something that does not belong to us because that is stealing. Now, I am going to give these two quarters to our office secretary to keep. So, if anyone lost two quarters they can get them from the office. Brenda (or any name), if no one claims them, then you can put them into the church offering. Let's bow our heads for a little prayer.

Prayer: Dear Lord, thank you for these boys and girls. Help us always to remember to be honest and never take something that belongs to someone else. In Jesus' name. Amen.

13

Boasting

Romans 12:3 ...Do not think of yourselves more highly than you ought ...NIV

Proverbs 27:2 Let another praise you, and not your own mouth; someone else, and not your own lips. NIV

Howdy boys and girls. I'm getting ready to go on vacation. We're going to the beach. I went to buy me a new bathing suit the other day. I was looking at them little bathing suits, and the store lady came up to me and said, "Do you want a one piece or a two piece suit?" I said, "Well, looking at the size of these, I better take a 10 piece."

Going on vacation reminds me of when I was in second grade. There was this boy named Edgar, who was always bragging about something. He was always bragging about going on vacation and going to the beach. If someone else said that they went to the beach, too. He would say, "Well, I bet we got to stay longer than you did, and I bet our beach was nicer than yours." Then he was always bragging about his clothes and his toys. I remember him saying that his football was nicer than any of the other boys' footballs. Then he was always bragging about how fast he could run. He said, "I can run faster than any of you because my shoes cost a lot of money." Well, he not only bragged all the time to us kids, but he was always bragging to the teacher, too. I think the teacher was like us kids. She was tired of hearing his bragging, too. She called it boasting. One day she taught a lesson about boasting from the Bible. She said that in Romans 12:3 it says that we are not to think of ourselves more highly than we should. She said that means to not get too puffed up in yourself. She said that if you think that you can really do something great, remember that there is always someone in the world that can do it better. She said that it is not nice to boast, and if she heard any of us kids boasting that she was going to stop us. Every day we would hear her say, "Edgar, stop your boasting." So Edgar ended up not talking too much after that 'cause I don't think that he knew how to talk without bragging about something.

I remember I got in trouble one time for boasting. When we ate corn on the cob at school, us kids would see who could eat the most rows off the cob at one time. I always won. My teeth went half way around that cob. I was dancing and said, "I won again." My teacher said, "Polly, don't boast." I said, "I'm sorry. I didn't mean to win. That's the way I always eat corn."

So, that's a good lesson to remember. Not to brag on ourselves but let other people brag on us and we brag on others. Remember that all of us are important in God's kingdom. Let's bow our heads for a little prayer.

Prayer: Dear Lord, thank you for the talents and blessings that you give to each of us. Please help us to never be boasting, but may we always realize that anything that we are able to do is only because of you. In Jesus' name we pray. Amen.

14

Wisdom

*Proverbs 9:10 The fear of the Lord is the
beginning of wisdom. NIV*

Howdy boys and girls. All of you probably remember my husband,
Henry. He is such a wise man. He went all the way through Fourth Grade.
Remember I told you that I only went through Second Grade. So that
means that Henry knows twice as much as I do. But, I went through that
second grade four times. Henry went through each grade twice. He said
that he did that so that he could learn twice as much. I think it worked
'cause he sure is wise. We sometimes go to a church where some of the
people don't speak to you part of the time. It don't bother me. But my
Henry, he is so wise. If someone doesn't speak to him, he goes over and
gets right up in their face and says, "Good morning. I don't think you
seen me back there, so I'm getting up closer so you can see me." He did
that a few times at church. Now everybody speaks to Henry. Everybody
makes sure they speak to Henry.

Do you boys and girls remember who the wisest man was in the
Bible? It was King Solomon. He was King David's son. The Bible says
that one night God appeared to Solomon and told him to ask for whatever
he wanted and He would give it to him. How would you like that to
happen to you? Solomon asked for wisdom to lead the people of Israel.

I think Solomon was pretty wise to start with to give God such a good and unselfish answer. God blessed him with more wisdom than anyone. God was so pleased with Solomon's request. God said, "Since you didn't ask for riches or honor, but asked for wisdom to govern my people, not only will I give you wisdom and knowledge, but I will also give you more riches and honor than any king before you or after you." That story is in 1Kings chapter 3. The Bible says that Solomon was so wise that men of all nations came to listen to his wisdom.

Solomon wrote thousands of songs and proverbs. In the Bible, in his book of Proverbs, he wrote several chapters about wisdom. He said in Proverbs 9:10 that the fear of the Lord is the beginning of wisdom. This doesn't mean that we have to be afraid of God because we know that God loves us. You can compare it with how you feel about your own Daddys. You love your Daddy and you are not afraid of him. You love your Daddy so much that you don't want to do anything to displease him. The only fear you have is the fear that you would see disappointment on your Daddy's face if you do something that you shouldn't; and maybe if it's something real bad, you may get punished. That is what Solomon meant. That we should love the Lord, our Heavenly Father, so much that we should be afraid of doing something to displease Him. That is why we want to keep the ten commandments. Solomon said that only fools despise wisdom and instructions.

So, now you boys and girls know how you can begin to have wisdom. Obey the Lord; obey your parents and your teachers. Maybe someday you will be as wise as my Henry. Wouldn't that be great? Let's bow our heads for a little prayer.

Prayer: Dear Lord, please fill us with wisdom so that we can please you in every way. In Jesus' name we pray. Amen.

15

Lent and Misunderstandings

Matthew 4:2 After fasting forty days and forty nights, he was hungry. NIV

Howdy boys and girls. Have you ever misunderstood what somebody said? You thought they said one thing, but they said something else. I don't know if it is that they don't talk plain or we don't hear good. But sometimes things get all mixed up between one person's mouth and another person's ears. It's just like the little girl who had a grandmother named Grace. One morning in church they were singing the song, "Amazing Grace," and the little girl asked her mother what was the amazing thing that her Grandmother Grace did. Of course, the song was not talking about the little girl's grandmother but it was talking about God's saving grace towards us. But you can understand how that little girl with a grandmother named Grace could get that confused 'cause I'm sure that she thought her Grandma was amazing anyway.

It's just like my husband, Henry. You boys and girls remember Henry. I showed you his picture the last time I was here. He's a handsome thing isn't he? Well Henry—I don't know if he can't hear good or he just can't hear me. But sometimes things get all mixed up between my mouth and his ears. The other day, Henry was watching a ballgame on TV. I was in the kitchen and he hollered at me and said,

"My team's winning." I said, "What team is it?" He answered, "It's 3 o'clock." I said, "I know that; I asked what was the name of your team." He said, "Oh, I thought you said what time is it?" So Henry is always misunderstanding me.

Right now it is Lent Season. That's why I'm going to tell you this story this morning. I'm going to tell you boys and girls about a big misunderstanding I made when I was in second grade. Well, my Sunday School teacher told us kids that it was the time of Lent, and she told us to decide what we wanted to give up for Lent and to bring it with us the next Sunday. Well, I thought she said lint and I knew that we were always getting lint on our clothes off of our blankets and our sweaters got those little fuzzy lint balls on them. So, I didn't say anything to my Mama. I just decided that week to take off all of those little lint balls off of all of our sweaters and put them in a paper poke—that's a paper bag. Then, I got a lot of lint off of the blankets until I had a bag full of lint. We didn't have clothes dryers back then or I could really have gotten a lot of lint out of the lint trap. But, our clothes dryer then was just a rope between two poles in the back yard. Anyway, on the next Sunday morning, I took my bag of lint to church and gave it to my Sunday School teacher and said, "Here is my lint." She looked real puzzled and then she said, "Polly, I think that you misunderstood. I didn't say lint, but I said lent." The other kids started laughing at me. I was so embarrassed. Then the teacher asked the other kids what they had brought for Lent and nobody had brought anything. Our teacher then went on to explain want Lent is. She said that it is a forty-day period before Easter. It starts on Ash Wednesday and we don't count Sundays. She said that this is a time when we really search ourselves to see if we have any sin in our lives and then repent of that sin by asking God to forgive us. It is a time when we prepare for Easter and remember that Jesus died on the cross for our sins. We observe Lent for 40 days because Jesus spent 40 days in the wilderness fasting and praying before He began His ministry. Lent is a time when many people fast and pray to become closer to God. She said that people often give up certain things or foods during Lent. Then my wonderful teacher said, "It looks like Polly was the only one who is giving up anything for Lent. Polly gave up a lot of her time that she could have spent playing, but instead she used her time to clean the lint off of the sweaters and blankets, which was very helpful to her mother. So, Polly, you definitely receive a star for today." That sure made me feel a lot better. The other kids weren't laughing then.

So, boys and girls, now you know what Lent season means. It has nothing to do with the lint on your clothes. Lent Season this year started on (date) and ends on (date). You boys and girls may want to think of something that you could give up for the remainder of Lent, something that would be a sacrifice—maybe candy or cookies—maybe playing your video games. Then you could spend that time studying the Bible instead of playing your games. But, that's between you and God and it's your decision.

You boys and girls have a wonderful Easter. I'm getting ready for Easter. I asked Henry if he thought that I should get a new hat for Easter. He said, "Why don't you just stick an Easter lily in that one." I said, "That's a good idea." So, that's what I did. That Henry sure is a wise man. Let's bow our heads for a little prayer.

Prayer: Dear Lord, thank you for your son, Jesus, who died for our sins. We pray that during this time of Lent that we will grow closer to you. In Jesus' name we pray. Amen.

16

Busybodies

2 Thessalonians 3:11 We hear that some among you are idle. They are not busy; they are busybodies. NIV

Howdy boys and girls. Do you boys and girls have telephones in your house? The first time I had a telephone was after me and Henry got married. We had what they called a party telephone line. I don't know why they called it a party. No one ever celebrated or brought us a cake or anything. But some of our neighbors were on our phone line, and we would know who the call was for by how many times the phone rang. The man from the phone company said, "Polly, you are two short." I said, "What do you mean, I'm too short. I'm five feet and seven inches tall." He said, "No, I mean that when the phone rings two short rings that it is for you. Otherwise, you don't have to pick up the phone." Well, my neighbor's ring was two longs and I kept getting them mixed up. When I heard the phone ring two times, I just picked it up. One day the phone rang twice, so, I picked it up and said, "Hello." My neighbor, Mr. Smith, said, "Polly, is that you on there? This call is for me because it was two long rings." I said, "Well, I thought it was two short rings. Who is calling anyway?" Then I heard a voice saying, "This is the sheriff." I said, "Okay, Mr. Smith, you can have this call." He said, "You can hang up now, Polly." So, I hung the phone up, but then I picked it back up again. I could hear everything that was being said. After that, whenever the phone rang, no matter how many rings it was, I picked it up and listened. I got to hear all kinds of things about my neighbors.

When Henry came home from work, I started telling him all of these things about our neighbors. He said, "Polly, where did you learn all of this stuff?" I said, "I heard it on the telephone." He said, "Polly, are you telling me that you eavesdropped on our neighbor's conversations?" I said, "Well, I guess you could call it eavesdropping." He said, "Polly, that is terrible. Those conversations are private and God doesn't want you listening in." I said that I looked through the Bible and I didn't see anything about not eavesdropping. It's just not in the Bible.

Henry left the room and in a few minutes came back with his Bible. Henry said, "I'm reading in 2Thessalonians 3:11 that Paul said that he doesn't want us to be busybodies. Do you think that you were being a busybody when you were listening on the phone?" I said, "Well, it was keeping me pretty busy picking up that phone all the time." Then Henry explained to me that a busybody is someone who is nosy or meddles in other people's business. My Henry is so wise. So, I told Henry that I was sorry and that I wouldn't listen in on our neighbors' calls anymore, and I didn't.

So, if you boys and girls see two adults, like your teachers, talking privately, should you go up and listen to what they are saying? No, that is being nosy or being a busybody. Paul said that we are to keep busy doing good things and not be busybodies. Let's bow our heads for prayer.

Prayer: Dear Lord, help us to not be busybodies, but be busy doing good works for you. In Jesus name we pray. Amen.

17

Hypocrites

Matthew 23: 27.28 "Woe to you, teachers of the law and Pharisees, you hypocrites! You are like whitewashed tombs, which look beautiful on the outside but on the inside are full of dead men's bones and everything unclean. In the same way, on the outside you appear to people as righteous but on the inside you are full of hypocrisy and wickedness.

Howdy boys and girls. This morning I want to tell you about our cat. First, I'll show you pictures of my whole family. There's me and Henry. There's our son, Odbert. His nickname is Odd. Everyone calls him Odd. There's our daughter, Sadie. Her nickname is Sad. There's our beautiful cat. Everyone says that she looks a lot like all of us. I think she fits into our family real well. We call her Rover, 'cause she always pretends to be a dog. She will try to bark like a dog. She even confuses some of the dogs in our neighborhood. She likes to chase rabbits. So we figured if she wanted to pretend that she was a dog that we would just go along with it and give her a dog's name. So she is Rover.

One time the preacher came to visit and he saw Rover. I told him the story of how our cat was always pretending to be a dog. He said our cat reminded him of a lot of people in his church. I said, "Do they pretend to be dogs?" He said, "No, they pretend to be Christians." He said that they come to Church on Sunday morning all dressed up and looking like Christians, but during the week they are doing everything they shouldn't. Some of them are lying and stealing. Some of them are acting mean to their neighbors. Some are cheating on their wives. Some are always quarreling and fighting. He said that in Matthew chapters 6 and 23, Jesus talked about those kind of people that pretend to be Christians but aren't. Jesus called them hypocrites.

I said, "I see what you mean, Preacher, but there is one thing different between my cat and the people in your church." He said, "What's that, Miss Polly?" I said, "Well, Rover can never change into a dog. She will always be a cat. But those people in your church can change into Christians if they want to. If they would go to the altar and ask God to forgive them and let Jesus direct their lives, then they could be Christians."

He said, "Miss Polly, you are absolutely right. We will pray for them." About that time, Rover came over and rubbed against the Preacher's leg and looked up at him and said, "Meow." I guess she didn't want to pretend around the preacher. With him, she just wanted to be herself.

So, let's remember, boys and girls, that we never want to just pretend that we are Christians; but we want to make sure that we are Christians. We do that by asking Jesus into our hearts and always trying to please him. Let's bow our heads for a little prayer.

Dear Lord, please come into our hearts and direct our lives so that we can be real Christians. In Jesus' name, Amen.

18

Complaining

Philippians 2:14 Do everything without complaining or arguing. NIV

Colossians 3:23 Whatever you do. work at it with all your heart. as working for the Lord. not for men. NIV

Howdy, boys and girls. I am a little upset this morning. On my way here, someone asked me if I was wearing my Halloween costume. I said no, this is my church-going outfit that I wear every Sunday. You boys and girls know that I always dress up nice like this and always try to look my best on Sundays. I asked her, "Why would you ask such a question?" She just looked kind of funny and said she was sorry. So, I'm not going to let her ruin my day. I'm just going to keep on praising the Lord and forget about what she said.

This morning I want to tell you about my and Henry's beautiful daughter. There's her picture. A lot of people thinks that she looks a lot like me. I can't really see that. Her name is Sadie. Her nickname is Sad. When she was a baby, people used to look at her and say, "That is sad." So we just nicknamed her Sad and it's short for Sadie. I see the guys out there looking at her. She's still single, guys.

Sad had chores to do at home. Her main chore was to wash the dishes after supper. One evening, I didn't hear any water splashing. So, I hollered into the kitchen and said, "Sad, are you washing the dishes?" She hollered back and said, "Yes, I'm almost done." I went into the kitchen and you won't believe what she was doing. She was letting the cat wash the dishes. That cat was just licking away on those plates. I yelled at her. I said, "Sadie Ann Wally—I always used her full name when I was upset—I cannot believe this. What is wrong with you? This is terrible. I can't believe that you would have the cat licking our dishes. Don't you know that is liable to make the cat sick?" Luckily, it didn't. The cat was okay. It missed some of the spots on the dishes anyway. I told Sadie that she would have to wash all of the dishes in the sink. She was complain'n, saying how she hated to wash dishes, and she didn't want to wash dishes. She just kept on complain'n. So I went and got my Bible, and I read her the scripture from Philippians 2:14 that says that we are to do everything without complaining or arguing. Also, Colossians 3:23 says, "Whatever you do, work at it with all your heart, as working for the Lord." I think that she thought about those verses because a little later I heard her singing "Jesus Loves Me" while she finished the dishes, and she never complained about washing the dishes anymore.

So, if you boys and girls ever feel like complain'n that you don't like to do your homework, or don't like cleaning your room, or doing any of your chores, remember those Bible verses. Remember that God doesn't want us complain'n; and whatever we do, think of doing it for the Lord, and it will make you feel a lot better. Let's bow our heads for a little prayer.

Prayer: Dear Lord, please help us to do our very best at whatever job we have to do, and please help us to do the job without complain'n. In Jesus' name we pray. Amen.

19

Birthday Present For Jesus

Matthew 25:40 The King will reply, 'I tell you the truth, whatever you did for one of the least of these brothers of mine, you did for me.' NIV

Howdy boys and girls. Christmas is a comin' soon. I'm just about ready for Christmas. I put this Christmas flower in my hat. I was goin' to wear that big cow bell like I did last year, but I couldn't catch Bessie, my cow. Either she'd getting faster or I'm getting slower. I chased her all over that hillside and I couldn't catch her. So, I wore this jingle bell instead.

I want to tell you boys and girls what it was like for Christmas when I was a little girl. We always had a real Christmas tree. We didn't have one of those artificial ones. My Mama and Papa would go out to the woods behind our house and cut down a pine tree about this high (measuring above your head). If there weren't any that short, he would cut the top out of a tall tree. We'd take it home and put it in the living room. We'd decorate it with lights and "ornarayments." I think that's the word. That's one of those big words that gets all tangled up around my teeth. Then we would cover that tree with those silver icicles. It looked like it had rained aluminum foil on our tree. We'd put a star on the top of the tree. Mama would spread a white sheet under the tree. Then we'd put a nativity scene on the sheet. It was made of cardboard and you stood up the figures. There was Joseph, Mary, the shepherds, the wise men, and the animals. Then little baby Jesus was in the center laying in a manger. Then Mama would tell us the story of why we celebrate Christmas. She said that Jesus, who is God's Son was born in Bethlehem and his Mom laid him in a manger because they didn't have anywhere else to stay that night. The angels appeared to the shepherds and told them about Jesus being born, so they went to visit Jesus. Also, the Wise Men came to see Jesus and brought Him expensive gifts.

I liked to look at little baby Jesus and I would get a warm feeling here in my heart. I told my Mama that I would like to give Jesus a present for Christmas, since it was his birthday. I had saved up a whole dollar and I told her that I wanted to give it to Jesus but I didn't know how. She told me to pray about it and maybe God would show me what to do.

The next Sunday when I went to church, there was a Christmas tree up on the platform but there wasn't anything on it. Our Sunday School Superintendent got up and said that the church was going to give our preacher the Christmas tree and he wanted us to cover it with dollar bills, so we could give the preacher a money tree for Christmas. Our preacher had four churches and he would come to our church and preach at 11 o'clock. Our preacher had a wife and three children and he was poor because the churches didn't pay him very much money 'cause they were all small churches. I decided that I would put my dollar on the tree for the preacher. We fastened the dollar bills on the tree with paper clips.

Then when the preacher arrived, Mr. Felton, our Superintendent, told the preacher that the Christmas tree covered with dollar bills was his Christmas present from the church. You should have seen that preacher's face. He was so surprised. He had tears in his eyes and he said, "I appreciate this so much. My family and I did not have any money for Christmas, but now you have just made this the best Christmas ever." I got that warm feeling here in my heart again and I remembered Jesus' words in Matthew chapter 25 that says that when we give to someone in need that it is the same as giving to Jesus. I realized that I had just given Jesus his birthday present.

Mr. Felton had also put some candy canes on the tree. So, our preacher said, "You have all been so good to me. I want to share something with you." Then he asked all of the children to come up front and he gave each of us a candy cane. That's what I am going to give each of you this morning. I hope that all of you have a very Merry Christmas. You may want to help someone in need this Christmas and that is a way of giving Jesus a birthday present. Let's bow our heads for prayer.

Prayer: Dear Lord, please show us who we can help this Christmas, so that we can give Jesus his birthday present. In Jesus' name we pray. Amen.

20

Lying

Proverbs 12:22 The Lord detests lying lips, but he delights in men who are truthful. NIV

Howdy boys and girls. When I get dressed every Sunday morning, can you guess who my role model is? She is a very classy dresser. Who do you think that I dress like? I'll tell you. My role model is Queen Elizabeth, as you can probably tell. The Queen and me always wear a hat. And notice the gloves, the Queen and me always wear gloves. We always try to look our best when we come to church. I may never get to meet the Queen, but someday I plan to meet our King. That is King Jesus, who is King of Kings. In order to meet Jesus someday, we must be sure that we have asked Jesus into our hearts and are trying to live our lives to please Him. One of the ways that we can please Jesus is to always be truthful.

When I was in second grade, there was a boy in our school named Claude who could never tell the truth. If he caught a fish that was ten inches long, he would tell everyone that the fish was at least thirty inches long. One day, he was telling the class that over the summer he and his parents had taken a trip to China. Our teacher, Miss Wilson, overheard him and told him that she would like for him to give a report the next day in front of the class about his trip. The next day, Claude said that he forgot and didn't have his report ready. The next day, he said the same thing.

The teacher then thought something was wrong. So, she called Claude's parents. They told the teacher that they had not been to China, but had eaten once at a Chinese Restaurant. The next day the teacher taught a lesson on being truthful. She said that sometimes people lie to just try to get attention, but in the end they always get caught and the attention that they receive is not good. She picked up her Bible and read Proverbs 12: 22. "The Lord detests lying lips, but he delights in men who are truthful." She encouraged the class to always tell the truth and to never stretch the truth. Claude was embarrassed that he had been caught telling a lie and he was more truthful after that.

So, boys and girls, let's remember that it is very important that we always tell the truth and that is one of the best ways that we can please King Jesus.

Prayer: Dear Lord, please help us to always let our lips speak words of truth. In Jesus' name we pray. Amen.

LaVergne, TN USA
27 August 2010
194927LV00008B/184/P